DINOSAURS! My First Book About CARNIVORES

To my best friend, Alex.
We may be an ocean apart, but you and
your family will always be my family. —G.B.

Interior and Cover Designer: Stephanie Sumulong
Art Producer: Janice Ackerman
Editor: Kristen Depken
Production Editor: Mia Moran

Illustrations © 2020 Annalisa & Marina Durante

Illustrator Photo © 2020 Fredi Marcarini

ISBN: Print 978-1-64611-429-0 | eBook 978-1-64611-603-4

R0

DINOSAURS! My First Book About CARNIVORES

"Dinosaur George" Blasing

Illustrations by Annalisa and Marina Durante

R

ROCKRIDGE
PRESS

ALL ABOUT CARNIVORES!

Dinosaurs are some of the most amazing animals that ever lived. **Paleontologists** are the scientists who dig up and study the **fossils** of plants and animals that lived a long time ago. They have discovered over 700 different kinds of dinosaurs—none more exciting than the carnivores!

A **carnivore** is an animal that eats only meat. Carnivorous dinosaurs are called **theropods**. Paleontologists can tell what a dinosaur ate by the shape of its teeth and claws. Sharp, pointy teeth could cut into meat. Sharp, curved claws could grip and hold **prey**. Thanks to their research, we know there were many different kinds of theropods. The smallest was the size of a house cat, and the largest was

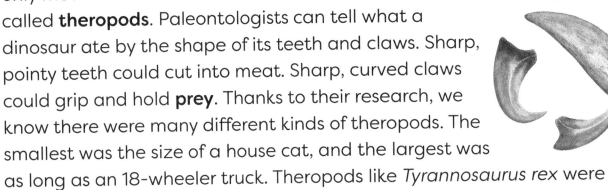

as long as an 18-wheeler truck. Theropods like *Tyrannosaurus rex* were tall enough to look through an upstairs window of a two-story house!

Theropods may look scary, but these meat-eating dinosaurs were not mean or nasty. They played an important role in nature. Without carnivores, there would have been too many plant eaters. They would have eaten all the plants!

2

DINOSAUR TIME

Did you know that not all dinosaurs lived at the same time? The first dinosaurs lived about 245 million years ago. These early dinosaurs were small, but over time dinosaurs became the largest animals that ever walked the Earth. The Age of Dinosaurs is called the Mesozoic Era. This era is divided into three time periods. Different kinds of dinosaurs lived in each one.

TRIASSIC PERIOD

When dinosaurs first lived on Earth. This period began 251 million years ago and lasted until 201 million years ago.

JURASSIC PERIOD

From 201 million to 145 million years ago. This period is sometimes called the Age of Giants because some of the largest dinosaurs, the **sauropods**, grew to huge sizes during this time.

CRETACEOUS PERIOD

From 145 million to 66 million years ago. Some of the most famous dinosaurs—like *Velociraptor*, *Triceratops*, and *Tyrannosaurus rex*—lived during this time period.

Carnivores lived during all three time periods. In this book we'll look at 30 of the most interesting theropods that ever lived.

We know a lot about these dinosaurs. But new discoveries are happening all the time, and what we know is always changing. Maybe one day you will make a new discovery and add another dinosaur to the list. The fossils are out there, waiting to be found!

Herrerasaurus had five toes (but only walked on three), and *Eoraptor* had five fingers.

Herrerasaurus had a flexible joint in its lower jaw that let it slide back and forth.

Eoraptor had claws that helped it run on sand, mud, or hard ground.

HERRERASAURUS

SAY IT! Huh-RARE-uh-SAWR-us

EORAPTOR

SAY IT! EE-oh-RAP-tur

Length: 13 feet

Height: 5.5 feet

Weight: 700 pounds

When: Late Triassic: 228 to 216 million years ago

Where: the forests of Argentina in South America

It ate: *Eoraptor* and large reptiles

It was the size of: a lion

Length: 3 feet

Height: 2 feet

Weight: 20 pounds

When: Late Triassic: 228 to 216 million years ago

Where: the forests of Argentina in South America

It ate: insects, fish, lizards, and eggs

It was the size of: a turkey

During the Late Triassic Period, *Herrerasaurus* was the largest meat-eating dinosaur on Earth! They were large **predators** that could take on almost any prey, including the *Eoraptor*. A small but fast hunter, *Eoraptor* may have hunted at night so it could sneak up on its prey. It also used the darkness to hide from *Herrerasaurus*.

COELOPHYSIS

Paleontologists know a lot about *Coelophysis* because dozens of skeletons were found in a place called Ghost Ranch in New Mexico. This "dinosaur **graveyard**" was created when a large **pack** of *Coelophysis* were crossing a flooded stream. Adults and babies were found at this site, proving that these dinosaurs lived in family groups. One skeleton had the bones of a baby crocodile in its stomach—its last meal!

Length: 10 feet

Height: 3 feet

Weight: 40 pounds

When: Late Triassic/Early Jurassic: 228 to 196 million years ago

Where: the forests of Arizona and New Mexico, and possibly Africa

It ate: insects, fish, reptiles, and eggs

It was the size of: a great white shark

Coelophysis had a wishbone, like a bird.

Coelophysis went to space! In 1998, the crew of the Space Shuttle *Endeavour* took a *Coelophysis* skull into space with them.

It was the fastest animal in its environment.

COMPSOGNATHUS

SAY IT! COMP-soh-NAY-thus

When the *Compsognathus* was first discovered, many people thought it was the smallest dinosaur, but they discovered later that those first bones found were from a baby. As adults, *Compsognathus* were dangerous carnivores that may have hunted in packs and eaten animals that washed ashore on the beaches they lived near.

Paleontologists once thought this dinosaur had two fingers, but it actually had three.

One *Compsognathus* fossil was found with the skeleton of a small lizard in its stomach!

Length: 4 feet

Height: 2 feet

Weight: 20 pounds

When: Late Jurassic: 155 to 145 million years

Where: the shores and forests of Europe

It ate: insects, fish, small reptiles, eggs, and baby dinosaurs

It was the size of: a turkey

GUANLONG

SAY IT! Gwan-LONG

Guanlong was a relative of *Tyrannosaurus rex*, but it lived 92 million years earlier. The name *Guanlong* means "crown dragon" after the large **crest** on its head, which would have been brightly colored on the males to attract a **mate** or threaten a rival.

It may have been covered in small, fuzzy feathers that helped it stay warm.

Guanlong could lose and regrow its teeth over and over again, like sharks do today!

Unlike the *T. rex*, *Guanlong* had three fingers instead of two.

Length: 10 feet

Height: 4 feet

Weight: 200 pounds

When: Late Jurassic: 161 to 155 million years

Where: the forests of China

It ate: other dinosaurs and reptiles

It was the size of: a tiger

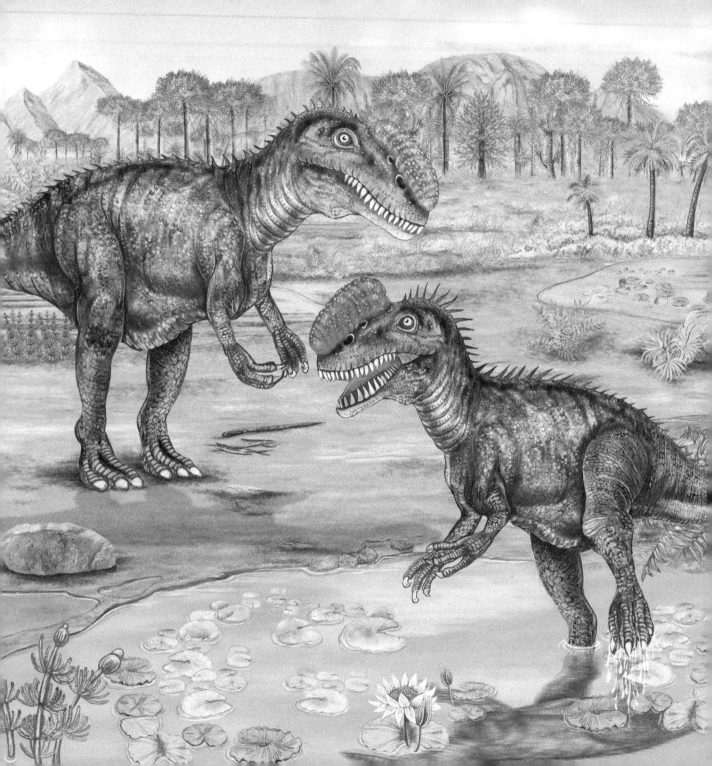

MONOLOPHOSAURUS

SAY IT! MON-uh-LOAF-oh-SAWR-us

Monolophosaurus means "single-crested lizard." It was named for the large, hollow crest on the top of its skull. Some scientists think the crest helped with its sense of smell, but others think they used it to attract a mate or threaten a rival. This medium-sized predator most likely hid in trees and bushes until a plant-eating dinosaur walked by—and then pounced on its prey!

Length: 16.5 feet

Height: 4 feet tall

Weight: 1,000 pounds

When: Middle Jurassic: 167 to 161 million years ago

Where: the forests of China

It ate: lizards, fish, and small and medium dinosaurs

It was the size of: a beluga whale

Monolophosaurus had long arms with sharp, curved claws on each hand.

Its stiff tail helped it change directions quickly when running at top speed.

There were more teeth on its top jaw than its bottom jaw.

CRYOLOPHOSAURUS

Cryolophosaurus means "frozen crested reptile." This carnivore was discovered in Antarctica, which is cold and frozen today but had parts that were warmer and covered in forests during the Age of Dinosaurs. *Cryolophosaurus* had a strange crest on its head. Scientists aren't sure what it was used for, but it was thin and fragile, so they know it wasn't used for battle. *Cryolophosaurus* was the top predator in its area.

Length: 20 feet

Height: 7 feet

Weight: 1,000 pounds

When: Early Jurassic: 189 to 183 million years ago

Where: the forests of Antarctica

It ate: small mammals, flying reptiles, and young sauropods

It was the size of: a truck

Cryolophosaurus was one of the largest predators on Earth during the time it lived.

It had a tiny brain, which means it was not a very smart dinosaur.

Bite marks on some bones show that these dinosaurs ate each other!

DILOPHOSAURUS

Dilophosaurus had two crests that ran along the top of its skull from its nose to its eyes. Because it had thin, light bones and arms that couldn't move much, this carnivore used its jaws and teeth to catch prey like fish and small animals.

A strange hook on its upper jaw may have helped hold slippery prey like fish.

Its upper teeth were almost twice as long as its lower teeth.

Length: 23 feet

Height: 5 feet

Weight: 880 pounds

When: Early Jurassic: 199 to 189 million years ago

Where: the forests of Arizona

It ate: fish, baby crocodiles, and small plant-eating dinosaurs

It was the size of: an SUV

CERATOSAURUS

SAY IT! Suh-RAT-oh-SAWR-us

Length: 23 feet

Height: 7 feet

Weight: 1,000 pounds

When: Late Jurassic:
155 to 150 million years ago

Where: the forests of Colorado and Utah, and possibly Tanzania in Africa

It ate: small and medium plant-eating dinosaurs and fish

It was the size of: a killer whale

ALLOSAURUS

SAY IT! AL-oh-SAWR-us

Length: 39 feet

Height: 16 feet

Weight: 6,000 pounds

When: Late Jurassic:
155 to 150 million years ago

Where: the forests of Colorado, New Mexico, Utah, Wyoming, and Portugal

It ate: small, medium, and large plant-eating dinosaurs

It was the size of: a city bus

Ceratosaurus and *Allosaurus* were two deadly giant carnivores. *Ceratosaurus* had a blade on its nose, a horn over each eye, and long, thin upper teeth that were perfect for slicing into prey. It had small pieces of bone in the skin of its back called **osteoderms** (OS-tee-oh-derms) that acted like body armor.

Allosaurus had powerful arms with three clawed fingers that could hold on to its prey while its teeth and jaws tore off large chunks of meat. It was large enough to attack an adult *Ceratosaurus*.

YANGCHUANOSAURUS

Yangchuanosaurus gets its name from Yangchuan, China, where it was found. It had long arms with three large claws and small horns over its eyes, and may have had very good eyesight. It was also large and fast, making it the most feared carnivore in the area.

Its long tail helped it balance. It could have been used as a weapon, too!

Yangchuanosaurus had **serrated** teeth that were used to cut meat.

Females protected their eggs by digging a nest and covering it with plants.

Length: 35 feet

Height: 10 feet

Weight: 5,000 pounds

When: Late Jurassic: 161 to 155 million years ago

Where: the forests of China

It ate: small, medium, and large plant-eating dinosaurs

It was the size of: a school bus

MEGALOSAURUS

SAY IT! MEG-uh-low-SAWR-us

Named in 1824, *Megalosaurus*, or "big reptile," was the first dinosaur to ever receive a name. At first, scientists thought *Megalosaurus* walked on four legs like a lizard or crocodile. But after more study, they discovered that it walked on its back legs. This dinosaur was a large, strong meat eater that could take on almost anything that lived in its **territory**.

Megalosaurus could catch its own food or steal the meals of smaller meat eaters.

To keep its claws sharp, *Megalosaurus* may have scratched trees, like bears and cats do today.

Strong neck muscles helped it pull pieces of meat off its prey.

Length: 30 feet

Height: 10 feet

Weight: 4,500 pounds

When: Middle Jurassic: 175 to 155 million years ago

Where: the forests and shores of England

It ate: medium and large plant-eating dinosaurs

It was the size of: a school bus

BAMBIRAPTOR

SAY IT! BAM-be-RAP-tur

Raptors were among the smartest and most dangerous meat-eating dinosaurs that ever lived. The family name for raptors is **dromaeosaurs** (droe-MAY-us-sawrs), and they came in all sizes. *Bambiraptor* was one of the smaller members of the raptor family. Paleontologists believe that *Bambiraptor* was covered in feathers like its modern cousins: hawks, eagles, and owls. It could jump down on unsuspecting prey!

Length: 3 feet

Height: 2 feet

Weight: 4 pounds

When: Late Cretaceous: 80 to 72 million years ago

Where: the forests and meadows of Montana

It ate: insects, eggs, small reptiles, and baby dinosaurs

It was the size of: a house cat

Bambiraptor slashed prey with a curved claw on its foot.

The first *Bambiraptor* was found in Montana by a 14-year-old boy who was hunting fossils!

It used its stiff tail for balance.

VELOCIRAPTOR

SAY IT! Vuh-LAH-su-RAP-tor

Velociraptor was one of the fastest members of the dromaeosaur family. These small but deadly dinosaurs may have hunted in packs to bring down larger prey. Even though it had feathers on its arms, *Velociraptor* was too heavy to fly. The feathers may have been used to keep warm at night.

Length: 6 feet

Height: 2 feet

Weight: 35 pounds

When: Late Cretaceous: 85 to 70 million years ago

Where: the deserts of Mongolia

It ate: small and medium plant-eating dinosaurs

It was the size of: a turkey

Like its bird cousins, *Velociraptor* had a wishbone!

Velociraptor only walked on two of its five toes—the others didn't touch the ground.

Its large, curved foot claw is called the "killing claw."

DEINONYCHUS

SAY IT! Dye-NON-ih-kus

Deinonychus was a fast, dangerous dinosaur that used the deadly curved claws on its feet to slice open its prey. It could hunt alone or in groups.

Its jaws were not very strong, so it used its hands to tear off pieces of meat.

Forward-facing eyes helped *Deinonychus* see and catch running prey.

Its tail was so stiff, it couldn't even wiggle it!

Length: 13 feet

Height: 3 feet

Weight: 150 pounds

When: Early Cretaceous: 118 to 110 million years ago

Where: the forests of Utah

It ate: plant-eating dinosaurs of all sizes

It was the size of: a tiger

UTAHRAPTOR

SAY IT! YOU-taw-RAP-tur

Utahraptor was the biggest and strongest of all raptors. It had powerful arms with long claws that could grab and shred its prey, and a curved foot claw that could slice through the thick skin of any dinosaur. Because it was so large and heavy, *Utahraptor* was not very fast.

Utahraptor is one of the oldest members of the raptor family.

Its curved foot claw was almost 15 inches long!

It's the official state dinosaur of Utah.

Length: 23 feet

Height: 8 feet

Weight: 250 pounds

When: Early Cretaceous: 118 to 110 million years ago

Where: the forests and beaches of Utah

It ate: medium and large plant-eating dinosaurs

It was the size of: an SUV

CONCAVENATOR

SAY IT! Con-CAVE-uh-nay-tor

One of the strangest meat eaters ever discovered, this medium-sized dinosaur had a large, pointy hump on its hips and bumps called quill knobs on its arms. The hump could have been used to help cool the *Concavenator* when it was hot, or to attract a mate. The quill knobs may have held long feathers that hung down from the arms. Paleontologists do not know for sure what these features were used for, but they do know that *Concavenator* was a very dangerous carnivore.

Concavenator laid eggs, like a bird.

It may have been able to run over 30 miles per hour!

It had three fingers on each hand.

Length: 20 feet

Height: 5 feet

Weight: 5,000 pounds

When: Early Cretaceous: 130 to 120 million years ago

Where: the lowlands and forests of Spain and Europe

It ate: small and medium plant-eating dinosaurs

It was the size of: an SUV

GALLIMIMUS

SAY IT! GAL-ee-MY-muss

Gallimimus was one of the fastest and smartest dinosaurs. Able to run up to 50 miles per hour, it could escape larger predators and chase down its prey. It ate mostly small reptiles, mammals, or eggs, but it may have eaten plants and fruit, too. But because *Gallimimus* had no teeth, it had to swallow whatever it ate whole. Because its arms were thin, it probably used its long neck to reach down and grab its prey.

Length: 20 feet

Height: 7 feet

Weight: 950 pounds

When: Late Cretaceous: 70 to 68 million years ago

Where: the deserts of Mongolia

It ate: small reptiles, mammals, baby dinosaurs, eggs, and plants

It was the size of: a truck

Gallimimus could deliver a deadly kick with its foot claws.

It swallowed small stones to help grind the food in its stomach.

It lived in herds for protection against larger meat eaters.

LABOCANIA

Labocania was a cousin of *Tyrannosaurus rex*, but it was not as large or powerful. It was fast, though, and able to chase down and catch its prey. Using its sharp teeth and long claws, *Labocania* could attack all but the biggest plant-eating dinosaurs.

It may have been striped or spotted to help it hide from its prey.

Labocania used its thick skull bones to knock down prey.

It had two fingers, like *T. rex.*

Length: 25 feet

Height: 6 feet

Weight: 3,000 pounds

When: Late Cretaceous: 83 to 70 million years ago

Where: the forests of Mexico

It ate: small and medium plant-eating dinosaurs

It was the size of: an elephant

RUGOPS

Rugops, or "wrinkle face," got its name because its strange skull was covered in bumps that made it look scary. Like its cousin the bird, a male *Rugops* probably had colorful markings on its head. Although it may have looked dangerous, this medium-sized carnivore had thin skull bones, a weak bite, and short arms, and probably didn't hunt its own prey. Instead, it would steal the food from smaller predators, or act like a **scavenger** by eating animals that were already dead.

Length: 17 feet

Height: 4 feet

Weight: 900 pounds

When: Late Cretaceous: 99 to 90 million years ago

Where: the coast of Niger in Africa

It ate: small and medium plant-eating dinosaurs

It was the size of: an SUV

Male *Rugops* may have had more bumps on their skulls than females.

It may have been able to change the color of its face when it was angry or scared.

Its teeth were short and peg-like.

CARNOTAURUS

SAY IT! CAR-no-TAW-rus

Carnotaurus, or "meat-eating bull," got its name from the large horns on its head—the largest and most powerful horns of any meat-eating dinosaur. *Carnotaurus* had short, weak arms, so it used its horns to knock down prey and then step on it to keep it from escaping. Once it captured its prey, *Carnotaurus* bit off chunks of meat that it swallowed whole. It also used its horns for battle.

Length: 26 feet

Height: 9 feet

Weight: 2,000 pounds

When: Late Cretaceous: 72 to 69 million years ago

Where: the forests of Argentina in South America

It ate: small, medium, and large plant-eating dinosaurs

It was the size of: a truck

Carnotaurus had tiny eyes and may have had poor vision.

Its skin was covered in thick, flat scales.

Carnotaurus had over 50 small but powerful teeth.

It had
58 long,
sharp teeth.

ALBERTOSAURUS

SAY IT! Al-BURT-oh-SAWR-us

Albertosaurus may have been the fastest of the large meat-eating dinosaurs. Its long legs would have allowed it to walk around 10 miles per hour. That's as fast as most kids can run! Paleontologists believe that these meat eaters lived and hunted in packs because they found 26 *Albertosaurus* skeletons in the same location in Canada. Because of its long legs and quick speed, it probably hid among the trees and then chased its prey, or worked with other family members to **ambush** it.

A two-year-old *Albertosaurus* was 6 feet long and weighed 110 pounds!

Albertosaurus had only two fingers on each hand.

Length: 30 feet

Height: 12 feet

Weight: 4,000 pounds

When: Late Cretaceous: 72 to 66 million years ago

Where: the forests of Canada and Montana

It ate: medium and large plant-eating dinosaurs

It was the size of: a school bus

BARYONYX

Baryonyx had huge claws, long and sharp teeth, and a head shaped like a crocodile's. *Baryonyx* is closely related to *Spinosaurus* and may have spent most of its time in the water, where it used its very large thumb claw to grab fish. Paleontologists know that *Baryonyx* ate fish because fish scales were found in its stomach area. So were the bones of a plant-eating dinosaur!

A hook-shaped snout helped it hold slippery fish in its mouth.

Baryonyx had 95 teeth, way more than most other meat eaters.

It may have been an excellent swimmer!

Length: 32 feet

Height: 8 feet

Weight: 2,700 pounds

When: Early Cretaceous: 140 to 112 million years ago

Where: near the lakes and rivers of Spain and England

It ate: fish, turtles, and small and medium plant-eating dinosaurs

It was the size of: a school bus

TARBOSAURUS

Tarbosaurus was the smaller cousin of *Tyrannosaurus rex*. It had powerful jaws and teeth—its bite was strong enough to crush bones! *Tarbosaurus* was heavy and probably couldn't run very fast, so it may have ambushed its prey instead of chasing it down. It could also steal prey from smaller meat eaters. Some paleontologists even believe *Tarbosaurus* was a scavenger that didn't hunt its prey at all.

Length: 33 feet

Height: 14 feet

Weight: 10,000 pounds

When: Late Cretaceous: 70 to 68 million years ago

Where: the forests of Mongolia and China

It ate: large plant-eating dinosaurs

It was the size of: a school bus

Tarbosaurus had an excellent sense of smell.

Its teeth curved backward to hold prey.

It was the largest theropod that lived in Asia.

DEINOCHEIRUS

SAY IT! Dye-no-KYE-rus

This dinosaur was strange! Its arms were almost eight feet long, and it had a long neck and tail and a large hump on its back. No one knows for sure what the hump was used for, but some paleontologists think it was used to store fat like the hump of a camel. *Deinocheirus* had a beak but no teeth, so it swallowed small stones called **gastroliths** to grind its food.

Length: 36 feet

Height: 16 feet

Weight: 14,000 pounds

When: Late Cretaceous: 70 to 68 million years ago

Where: along the rivers and lakes of Mongolia

It ate: fish, small and medium dinosaurs, and possibly plants

It was the size of: a school bus

Its claws were small but thick and good for digging.

Deinocheirus may have been an omnivore, eating both plants and meat.

Its main predator was *Tarbosaurus*.

Like its cousin *Allosaurus*, *Carcharodontosaurus* had three fingers on each hand.

CARCHARODONTOSAURUS

Carcharodontosaurus, or "shark-toothed lizard," got its name from its shark-like teeth, which could slice through even the thickest skin of any dinosaur. These sharp teeth—plus a powerful bite, strong neck, and sharp claws—allowed it to hunt the biggest of all dinosaurs: sauropods. *Carcharodontosaurus* also had a heavy body that was made for battle. When it attacked, it rushed in with its mouth open and grabbed its prey. It was one of the top hunters of Africa. Even giant meat eaters like *Spinosaurus* probably stayed away.

Carcharodontosaurus could lift almost 1,000 pounds in its jaws. That's as much as 4,000 hamburgers!

Its teeth were up to 8 inches long.

Length: 39 feet

Height: 11 feet

Weight: 15,000 pounds

When: Early to Late Cretaceous: 112 to 93 million years ago

Where: the forests of Algeria, Egypt, Morocco, and Niger

It ate: plant-eating dinosaurs of all sizes

It was the size of: a city bus

ACROCANTHOSAURUS

Acrocanthosaurus, or "high-spined lizard," gets its name from the large, raised ridge on its neck and back, which may have been used to make it look larger to rivals, or to cool down or warm up its body. *Acrocanthosaurus* is known as a head hunter because it caught its prey with its mouth, then used its claws to hold on to it. Fossils show that it hunted the sauropods.

Its teeth had sharp edges, like a steak knife, to slice its food.

Acrocanthosaurus reached its adult size by 12 years old.

The ridge on its back was almost 12 inches tall!

Length: 40 feet

Height: 12 feet

Weight: 12,000 pounds

When: Early Cretaceous: 125 to 99 million years ago

Where: the shores of Texas, Oklahoma, and Utah

It ate: medium and large plant-eating dinosaurs

It was the size of: a city bus

Tyrannosaurus rex may have been able to swallow 500 pounds of meat in each bite!

TYRANNOSAURUS

SAY IT! Tie-RAN-oh-SAWR-us

The name *Tyrannosaurus rex* means "tyrant lizard king." Nicknamed *T. rex*, it was the largest carnivore that ever lived in North America. It had the most powerful bite of any theropod, and its teeth were strong enough to crack even the largest bones. The only thing a *T. rex* feared was another *T. rex*. Females were larger than males, probably to protect their young, but males were probably faster and more brightly colored than females. Any dinosaur that lived in the territory of a *Tyrannosaurus* had to watch out for attack.

The pads on its feet could feel the footsteps of nearby plant-eating dinosaurs.

Its teeth were covered in bacteria. One bite would have caused a serious infection.

Length: 41 feet

Height: 12 feet

Weight: 15,000 pounds

When: Late Cretaceous: 66 to 65 million years ago

Where: near forests and rivers throughout western North America

It ate: anything it could catch!

It was the size of: a city bus

GIGANOTOSAURUS

The largest meat-eating theropod in South America, *Giganotosaurus* was even larger than *Tyrannosaurus*. Its thin teeth were perfect for slicing meat, but they were not strong enough to break bones, so *Giganotosaurus* probably bit into its prey and then waited for it to become too weak to fight back. Its rough, bumpy nose made it look wrinkled. This may have helped others of its kind recognize it. Its arms were longer than those of other large meat-eating dinosaurs but still short compared to its body. It only used them to hold the prey, not catch it.

It used its tail for balance and as a weapon.

Length: 43 feet

Height: 14 feet

Weight: 20,000 pounds

When: Late Cretaceous: 99 to 97 million years ago

Where: the forests of Argentina in South America

It ate: medium and large plant-eating dinosaurs

It was the size of: a city bus

CRETACEOUS

SPINOSAURUS

SAY IT! SPINE-oh-SAWR-us

Spinosaurus is the longest and tallest meat-eating dinosaur known. It had a large fin, or sail, on its back that was over five feet tall. The *Spinosaurus* spent a lot of time in the water, and its sail helped it stay warm by capturing the rays of the sun and heating its blood. *Spinosaurus* had a strange skull. Its long snout was lined with different-size teeth that ranged from as short as a LEGO to longer than a dinner fork. It ate fish and had a hook at the end of its snout that was perfect for grabbing them.

It was an excellent swimmer but could also hunt on land.

Length: 52 feet

Height: 16 feet

Weight: 25,000 pounds

When: Early to Late Cretaceous: 112 to 93 million years ago

Where: near the swamps, rivers, and lakes of Egypt, Morocco, and Africa

It ate: fish, turtles, snakes, and plant-eating dinosaurs

It was the size of: an 18-wheeler truck

CRETACEOUS

Glossary

ambush: To hide and then surprise prey

carnivore: An animal that eats only meat

crest: A bone connected to the head that can be brightly colored and even make sounds

dromaeosaurs: Also called raptors, these are meat-eating dinosaurs with curved claws on their feet

fossil: A plant or animal that has slowly been turned to stone by minerals in the ground

gastroliths: Rocks that are swallowed whole and then roll around in the stomach to grind up food, usually swallowed by animals that cannot chew their food with their mouths

graveyard: A location where more than one dinosaur skeleton has been found

mate: A dinosaur of the opposite sex that becomes the parent of offspring

omnivore: An animal that eats both plants and meat

osteoderms: Pieces of thick bone material attached to the outside of the skin that are used like body armor to protect the dinosaur from attack

pack: A group of three or more of the same species of meat-eating dinosaurs that work together to hunt prey

paleontologist: A scientist who digs up and studies fossils of plants and animals of the past

predators: Meat-eating animals that hunt living prey

prey: The food source of a meat eater or something that is hunted by others

raptors: Common name for dromaeosaurs

sauropods: The largest land animals that ever lived, these dinosaurs walked on four legs and had long necks and tails, and sometimes were called "long necks"

scavenger: An animal that eats things that were already dead

serrated: Covered with sharp, jagged points that help slice through meat

territory: The area or location that is claimed by a carnivore to be its own property

theropods: Meat-eating dinosaurs that walked on two legs

Index

About the Author

"Dinosaur George" Blasing is a self-taught paleontologist who has studied and excavated dinosaurs and other prehistoric life for more than 35 years. He is a public speaker, author, and television writer. He also owns a traveling dinosaur museum that brings the prehistoric world to young people and adults across the country.

In 2007, he co-created, wrote, and hosted a 12-part television series for the History Channel called *Jurassic Fight Club*. The series was shown in more than 25 countries and seen by over 30 million viewers. Although he enjoyed working for the History Channel, his true passion is teaching children. Since 1997, Dinosaur George has performed live to over 4 million students and adults throughout the United States and Canada, and has appeared at over 5,000 schools, museums, and public events.

Dinosaur George is also an animal behaviorist, studying modern animals and comparing their behavior to animals of the past. In his spare time, he hosts a podcast and social media pages.

He was born in Colorado but moved to Texas at an early age. He grew up on a farm near San Antonio, Texas, and loves the outdoors. When he's not digging up dinosaurs, hosting a podcast, or traveling with his museum, George enjoys camping, hiking, and being outdoors with nature. Visit him online at DinosaurGeorge.com.

About the Illustrators

Annalisa and **Marina Durante** are nature and science illustrators. They are twin sisters who have loved nature and animals since they were children. Marina enjoys hiking, deep-water diving, and photography. The photos she takes while exploring nature are the inspiration for her art. Annalisa is inspired by Eastern philosophy and enjoys meditating as she explores the outdoors.

In 2001, Marina and Annalisa were invited by the Galapagos National Park to draw the birds of the Galapagos Islands. They have worked for the Food and Agriculture Organization (FAO) of the United Nations, illustrating recently discovered species of fish. Their works have been published all over the world, and they have won a number of international art prizes. They especially enjoy illustrating portraits of animals and pets. Find them online at DuranteIllustrations.com.